Love

You'll find a variety of realistic and decorative Valentine ephemera pieces on the following pages. Maybe you're curious what you should do with them? Here are a couple of ideas:

Using them in your journal, planner and other fascinating projects. You can decorate invitations, make scrapbook designs, and make gift tags of your own. Your imagination is the only boundary.

Using the pictures to inspire your imagination.

Thank you for buying this book, and we hope you've had a nice time using it.

Createlt Studio

Check out more collections and follow us on Amazon:
https://www.amazon.com/CreateIt-Studio/e/B092LKZR2B

This little kitten,
Valentine,
Has come
to ask you

to be
mine.

To my Valentine

To my Valentine

Chanson à l'occasion du mariage de Mr. Le Comte de Massol avec Mademoiselle De jour!

Quand l'occasion nous engage
à suivre ses desirs
doit on pour être sage
se livrer aux plaisirs
  eh mais oui da
on ne trouver du mal a ça.

2.

Qu'Amour soit du voïage
et Les Ris et Les jeux
faut il dans son menage
badiner avec eux
  eh mais oui da
on ne trouver du mal a ça.

3.

D'une vertu sauvage
Loin de nous Les remords
ecoutons le bel age
et suivons ses transports
  eh mais oui da
on ne trouver du mal a ça.

4.

Ce sera Le systême
de nos epoux charmants
ils agiront de même
nous serons tous contents eh mais oui da &c.

5.

Après maintes jeux
viennent d'autres cadeaux
éteignent les bougies
et tirent les rideaux eh mais oui da &c.

6.

Et l'ardeur mutuelle
qu'inspirent leurs ébats
on oit qu'en la ruelle
l'occasion Ditoit tout bas eh mais oui da &c.

7.

Riche Dieu de la nopce
ne fais point de crédit
il faut en tout nepce
Ou comptant au Debit. eh mais oui da &c.

8.

J'y a de ta gloire de
Dans les tendres tournois
De seller la victoire
par de galants exploits eh mais oui da &c.

9.

Pour que ta flamme dure
et brille aux yeux de tous
fais leur bonne mesure
De tes feux les plus doux eh mais oui da &c.

10.

Pour couronner l'ouvrage
dans neuf mois tout au plus
qu'un poupon soit le gage
de tes voeux assidus
  eh mais oui da
on ne trouver du mal a ça.

Fin.

Love
you

Cutie
pie

With
love

Be
Mine

Hugs & Kisses

Hugs & Kisses

CUPID'S HEART

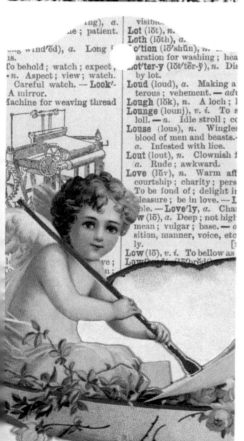

ev thy hope
be as fair.
Thy fortunes
as sweet

Because I love you

Because I love you

True Love!

Summer may change for winter,
Flowers may fade and die,
But I shall ever love thee
While I can heave a sigh!

All joys be thine.

Forget me not.

Life bear for you its sweetest flowers.

To:
_____

From:
_____

LOVE

To:
_____

From:
_____

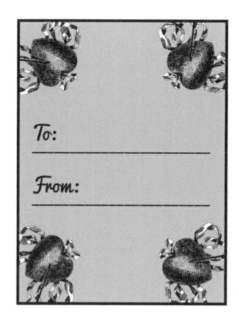

To:
_____

From:
_____

To:
_____

MY HEART
LOVES
YOU

From:
_____

To:
_____

From:
_____

To:
_____

I LOVE YOU
MORE AND MORE

From:
_____

DREAMING OF LOVE

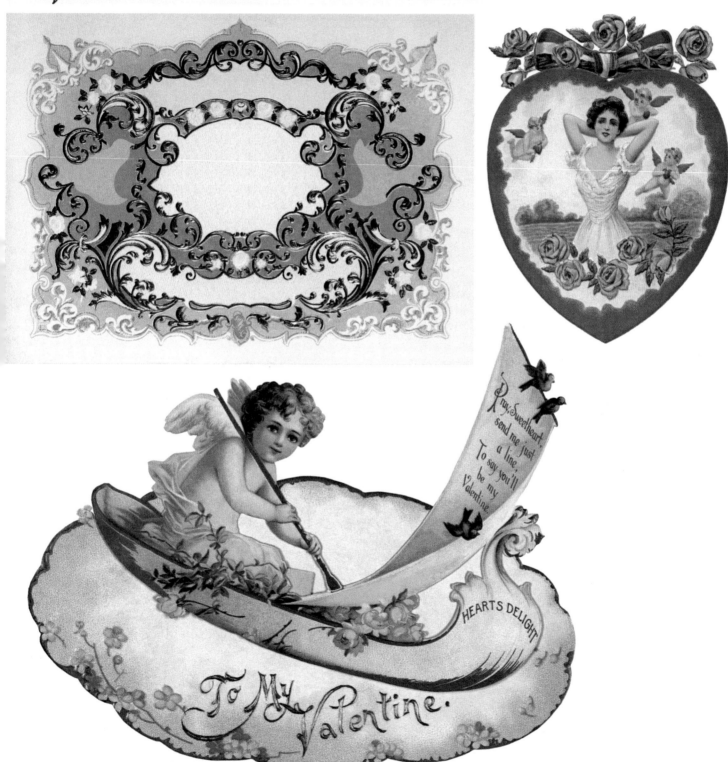

Pray, Sweetheart, send me just a line, To say you'll be my Valentine.

HEARTS DELIGHT

To My Valentine.

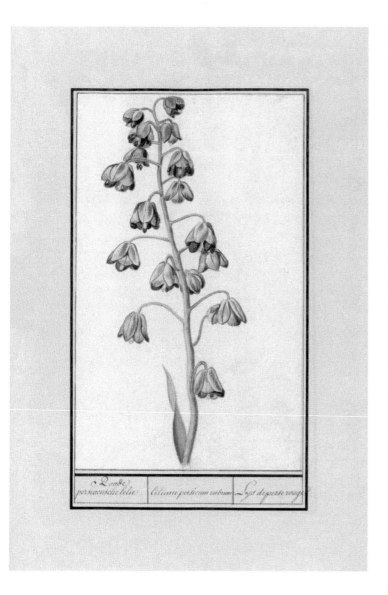

To my Valentine

To my Valentine!

To my VALENTINE.

My Love to You.

I LOVE YOU MORE AND MORE

"And then they rode to the divided way, there kiss'd, and parted weeping."

He finds her, and this is the consequence.

Made in the USA
Monee, IL
12 December 2024

73599455R00026